MW01013323

OUR
ADVENTURES

Copyright © 2018 by Megan Adams
. All rights reserved. This book or any portion thereof may not be re-
produced or used in any manner whatsoever without the express written
permission of the publisher.

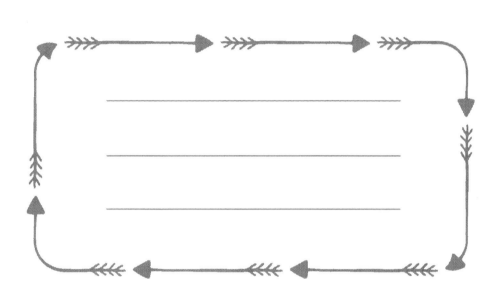

101 couples adventure ideas for inspiraton for your own list

1. Ride in a hot air balloon
2. Visit each other's home towns and give tours
3. Research and record your family trees
4. Learn how to say "I love you" in at least 5 languages
5. Go on an overnight train trip
6. Visit a haunted mansion
7. Visit a castle
8. Write a song together, even if it's silly and neither of you can sing
9. Create code words for party escapes, I love you's, having a bad day, or anything else
10. Grow a vegetable garden together
11. Go deep sea fishing or whale watching
12. Ride a tandem bicycle
13. Go to a remote island or location
14. Learn a new language together
15. Stay at a bed and breakfast
16. Kiss under a waterfall
17. Take an unplanned overnight road trip
18. Dance in the rain
19. Kiss on the top of a ferris wheel ride
20. Get a couples massage
21. Go bowling
22. Create a signature impressive meal together or take a cooking class together
23. Ride horses on the beach
24. Go to a nude beach
25. Go to a wine tasting
26. Pick your own fruit at an orchard and make something with it
27. Make life goals together
28. Write a love poem together or to each other
29. Try each other's hobbies
30. Wear matching outfits in public
31. Watch a meteor shower
32. Write cute sweet notes or texts weekly
33. Have a tradition for every holiday
34. Learn a line dance together or some other synchronized dance
35. Volunteer to do something together

101 couples adventure ideas for inspiraton for your own list

36.	Take dance lessons together
37.	Teach each other something
38.	Have sex in the water (ocean, pool, hot tub or shower)
39.	Make love in every room of your house
40.	Recreate your first date or proposal
41.	Hang out together in a hammock
42.	Go snorkeling
43.	Sing together – go Christmas caroling or do karaoke
44.	Go white water rafting
45.	Go camping and sleep in a tent
46.	Kiss in front of the Eiffel tower
47.	Say I love you in a gondola
48.	Swim with dolphins, stingrays or sharks
49.	Watch a volcano erupt
50.	See the northern lights
51.	Watch the sunrise and sunset in the same day
52.	Attend and bet on a horse race
53.	Get your palms or futures read
54.	Hunt for mushrooms
55.	Try the most exotic foods on the menu in a different country
56.	Meet each other for a date in disguise
57.	Donate blood together
58.	Attend a professional athletic event
59.	Feed each other gourmet desserts
60.	Visit every continent
61.	Complete a corn maze
62.	Go indoor skydiving
63.	Take a helicopter tour
64.	Attend a major festival or event (Mardi Gras, New Year's Eve, Burning Man)
65.	Spend a weekend away with no electronic devices
66.	Swim in every ocean
67.	Go bird watching
68.	Do tandem parasailing
69.	Get cartoon images drawn of yourselves
70.	Pack and go on a picnic
71.	Race go carts or bumper cars

101 couples adventure ideas for inspiraton for your own list

72. Stargaze somewhere amazing
73. Ride a river boat
74. Paddleboard or surf together
75. Relax in a hot springs
76. Go on a safari
77. Visit a cathedral
78. Complete a jigsaw puzzle together
79. Have a candlelight dinner for no reason
80. Try out local food trucks
81. Tour all of your local attractions
82. Watch a double feature movie matinee
83. Go bowling, roller skating or ice skating
84. Ride a mechanical bull
85. Go geocaching
86. Fly kites together
87. Get pedicures together
88. Play paintball or laser tag
89. Design your own plates at a pottery studio
90. Go to a local musical show, concert or play
91. Feed the ducks
92. Complete a crossword puzzle together
93. Go to a farmers market
94. Play strip poker
95. Build a sandcastle together
96. Learn a magic trick together
97. Rent a convertible
98. Attend an amazing fireworks display
99. Make your own wine, beer, cider, kombucha or create and name your own signatures beverage
100. Play at the playground of a loyal park
101. Skip rocks

Activity	Page	Done!
		☐
		☐
		☐
		☐
		☐
		☐
		☐
		☐
		☐
		☐
		☐
		☐
		☐
		☐
		☐
		☐
		☐
		☐
		☐
		☐

Activity	Page	Done!
		☐
		☐
		☐
		☐
		☐
		☐
		☐
		☐
		☐
		☐
		☐
		☐
		☐
		☐
		☐
		☐
		☐
		☐
		☐
		☐
		☐
		☐

Activity

Page   Done!

Activity

Page   Done!

Activity

Page   Done!

Date Completed: _____

Description:

_____

_____

_____

_____

_____

_____

Why we wanted to do this:

_____

_____

Thoughts/Memories:

_____

_____

_____

_____

_____

_____

_____

_____

_____

_____

_____

_____

_____

Date Completed: _____

Description:

_____

_____

_____

_____

_____

_____

Why we wanted to do this:

_____

_____

Thoughts/Memories:

_____

_____

_____

_____

_____

_____

_____

_____

_____

_____

_____

_____

Date Completed: _____

Description:

_____

_____

_____

_____

_____

_____

Why we wanted to do this:

_____

_____

Thoughts/Memories:

_____

_____

_____

_____

_____

_____

_____

_____

_____

_____

_____

_____

Date Completed: _____

Description:

_____

_____

_____

_____

_____

_____

Why we wanted to do this:

_____

_____

Thoughts/Memories:

_____

_____

_____

_____

_____

_____

_____

_____

_____

_____

_____

_____

Date Completed: _____

Description:

_____

_____

_____

_____

_____

_____

Why we wanted to do this:

_____

_____

Thoughts/Memories:

_____

_____

_____

_____

_____

_____

_____

_____

_____

_____

_____

_____

>>>————➤ >>>————➤   >>>————➤   >>>————➤

Date Completed: _____

Description:

_____
_____
_____
_____
_____
_____

Why we wanted to do this:

_____
_____

Thoughts/Memories:

_____
_____
_____
_____
_____
_____
_____
_____
_____
_____
_____

Date Completed: _____

Description:

_____

_____

_____

_____

_____

_____

Why we wanted to do this:

_____

_____

Thoughts/Memories:

_____

_____

_____

_____

_____

_____

_____

_____

_____

_____

_____

_____

>>>———➤ >>>———➤ >>>———➤ >>>———➤

Date Completed: _____

Description:

_____

_____

_____

_____

_____

_____

Why we wanted to do this:

_____

_____

Thoughts/Memories:

_____

_____

_____

_____

_____

_____

_____

_____

_____

_____

_____

_____

Date Completed: _____

Description:

_____

_____

_____

_____

_____

_____

Why we wanted to do this:

_____

_____

Thoughts/Memories:

_____

_____

_____

_____

_____

_____

_____

_____

_____

_____

_____

_____

Date Completed: _____

Description:

_____

_____

_____

_____

_____

_____

Why we wanted to do this:

_____

_____

Thoughts/Memories:

_____

_____

_____

_____

_____

_____

_____

_____

_____

_____

_____

_____

Date Completed: _____

Description:

_____

_____

_____

_____

_____

Why we wanted to do this:

_____

_____

Thoughts/Memories:

_____

_____

_____

_____

_____

_____

_____

_____

_____

_____

Date Completed: _____

Description:

_____

_____

_____

_____

_____

_____

Why we wanted to do this:

_____

_____

Thoughts/Memories:

_____

_____

_____

_____

_____

_____

_____

_____

_____

_____

_____

_____

Date Completed: _____

Description:

_____

_____

_____

_____

_____

Why we wanted to do this:

_____

_____

Thoughts/Memories:

_____

_____

_____

_____

_____

_____

_____

_____

_____

_____

_____

>>>———————➤ >>>———————➤ >>>———————➤ >>>———————➤

Date Completed: _____

Description:

_____

_____

_____

_____

_____

_____

Why we wanted to do this:

_____

_____

Thoughts/Memories:

_____

_____

_____

_____

_____

_____

_____

_____

_____

_____

_____

_____

Date Completed: _____

Description:

_____
_____
_____
_____
_____
_____

Why we wanted to do this:

_____
_____

Thoughts/Memories:

_____
_____
_____
_____
_____
_____
_____
_____
_____
_____
_____

Date Completed: _____

Description:

_____

_____

_____

_____

_____

_____

Why we wanted to do this:

_____

_____

Thoughts/Memories:

_____

_____

_____

_____

_____

_____

_____

_____

_____

_____

_____

Date Completed: _____

Description:

_____
_____
_____
_____
_____
_____

Why we wanted to do this:

_____
_____

Thoughts/Memories:

_____
_____
_____
_____
_____
_____
_____
_____
_____
_____
_____
_____

Date Completed: _____

Description:

_____

_____

_____

_____

_____

_____

Why we wanted to do this:

_____

_____

Thoughts/Memories:

_____

_____

_____

_____

_____

_____

_____

_____

_____

_____

_____

_____

>>>———➤ >>>———➤ >>>———➤ >>>———➤

Date Completed: _____

Description:

_____

_____

_____

_____

_____

_____

Why we wanted to do this:

_____

_____

Thoughts/Memories:

_____

_____

_____

_____

_____

_____

_____

_____

_____

_____

_____

Date Completed: _____

Description:

_____

_____

_____

_____

_____

_____

Why we wanted to do this:

_____

_____

Thoughts/Memories:

_____

_____

_____

_____

_____

_____

_____

_____

_____

_____

_____

_____

>>>———————● >>>———————● >>>———————● >>>———————●

Date Completed: _____

Description:

_____

_____

_____

_____

_____

_____

Why we wanted to do this:

_____

_____

Thoughts/Memories:

_____

_____

_____

_____

_____

_____

_____

_____

_____

_____

_____

Date Completed: _____

Description:

_____

_____

_____

_____

_____

_____

Why we wanted to do this:

_____

_____

Thoughts/Memories:

_____

_____

_____

_____

_____

_____

_____

_____

_____

_____

_____

_____

Date Completed: _____

Description:

_____

_____

_____

_____

_____

Why we wanted to do this:

_____

_____

Thoughts/Memories:

_____

_____

_____

_____

_____

_____

_____

_____

_____

_____

Date Completed: _____

Description:

_____

_____

_____

_____

_____

_____

Why we wanted to do this:

_____

_____

Thoughts/Memories:

_____

_____

_____

_____

_____

_____

_____

_____

_____

_____

_____

_____

Date Completed: _____

Description:

_____

_____

_____

_____

_____

_____

Why we wanted to do this:

_____

_____

Thoughts/Memories:

_____

_____

_____

_____

_____

_____

_____

_____

_____

_____

_____

_____

Date Completed: _____

Description:

_____

_____

_____

_____

_____

_____

Why we wanted to do this:

_____

_____

Thoughts/Memories:

_____

_____

_____

_____

_____

_____

_____

_____

_____

_____

_____

_____

_____

Date Completed: _____

Description:

_____
_____
_____
_____
_____

Why we wanted to do this:

_____
_____

Thoughts/Memories:

_____
_____
_____
_____
_____
_____
_____
_____
_____
_____
_____

Date Completed: _____

Description:

_____

_____

_____

_____

_____

_____

Why we wanted to do this:

_____

_____

Thoughts/Memories:

_____

_____

_____

_____

_____

_____

_____

_____

_____

_____

_____

_____

Date Completed: _____

Description:

_____

_____

_____

_____

_____

_____

Why we wanted to do this:

_____

_____

Thoughts/Memories:

_____

_____

_____

_____

_____

_____

_____

_____

_____

_____

_____

_____

>>> ———➤   >>> ———➤   >>> ———➤   >>> ———➤

Date Completed: _____

Description:

_____

_____

_____

_____

_____

_____

Why we wanted to do this:

_____

_____

Thoughts/Memories:

_____

_____

_____

_____

_____

_____

_____

_____

_____

_____

_____

_____

Date Completed: _____

Description:

_____

_____

_____

_____

_____

Why we wanted to do this:

_____

_____

Thoughts/Memories:

_____

_____

_____

_____

_____

_____

_____

_____

_____

_____

_____

Date Completed: _____

Description:

_____

_____

_____

_____

_____

_____

Why we wanted to do this:

_____

_____

Thoughts/Memories:

_____

_____

_____

_____

_____

_____

_____

_____

_____

_____

_____

_____

Date Completed: _____

Description:

_____

_____

_____

_____

_____

_____

Why we wanted to do this:

_____

_____

Thoughts/Memories:

_____

_____

_____

_____

_____

_____

_____

_____

_____

_____

_____

_____

Date Completed: _____

Description:

_____

_____

_____

_____

_____

_____

Why we wanted to do this:

_____

_____

Thoughts/Memories:

_____

_____

_____

_____

_____

_____

_____

_____

_____

_____

_____

_____

Date Completed: _____

Description:

_____

_____

_____

_____

_____

_____

Why we wanted to do this:

_____

_____

Thoughts/Memories:

_____

_____

_____

_____

_____

_____

_____

_____

_____

_____

_____

_____

Date Completed: _____

Description:

_____

_____

_____

_____

_____

_____

Why we wanted to do this:

_____

_____

Thoughts/Memories:

_____

_____

_____

_____

_____

_____

_____

_____

_____

_____

_____

_____

_____

Date Completed: _____

Description:

_____

_____

_____

_____

_____

_____

Why we wanted to do this:

_____

_____

Thoughts/Memories:

_____

_____

_____

_____

_____

_____

_____

_____

_____

_____

_____

_____

Date Completed: _____

Description:

_____

_____

_____

_____

_____

_____

Why we wanted to do this:

_____

_____

Thoughts/Memories:

_____

_____

_____

_____

_____

_____

_____

_____

_____

_____

_____

_____

Date Completed: _____

Description:

_____

_____

_____

_____

_____

Why we wanted to do this:

_____

_____

Thoughts/Memories:

_____

_____

_____

_____

_____

_____

_____

_____

_____

_____

_____

Date Completed: _____

Description:

_____

_____

_____

_____

_____

Why we wanted to do this:

_____

_____

Thoughts/Memories:

_____

_____

_____

_____

_____

_____

_____

_____

_____

_____

_____

Date Completed: _____

Description:

_____

_____

_____

_____

_____

_____

Why we wanted to do this:

_____

_____

Thoughts/Memories:

_____

_____

_____

_____

_____

_____

_____

_____

_____

_____

Date Completed: _____

Description:

_____

_____

_____

_____

_____

Why we wanted to do this:

_____

_____

Thoughts/Memories:

_____

_____

_____

_____

_____

_____

_____

_____

_____

_____

_____

_____

Date Completed: _____

Description:

_____

_____

_____

_____

_____

_____

Why we wanted to do this:

_____

_____

Thoughts/Memories:

_____

_____

_____

_____

_____

_____

_____

_____

_____

_____

_____

_____

Date Completed: _____

Description:

_____

_____

_____

_____

_____

_____

Why we wanted to do this:

_____

_____

Thoughts/Memories:

_____

_____

_____

_____

_____

_____

_____

_____

_____

_____

_____

_____

Date Completed: _____

Description:

_____
_____
_____
_____
_____
_____

Why we wanted to do this:

_____
_____

Thoughts/Memories:

_____
_____
_____
_____
_____
_____
_____
_____
_____
_____
_____

Date Completed: _____

Description:

_____

_____

_____

_____

_____

Why we wanted to do this:

_____

_____

Thoughts/Memories:

_____

_____

_____

_____

_____

_____

_____

_____

_____

_____

_____

_____

Date Completed: _____

Description:

_____

_____

_____

_____

_____

_____

Why we wanted to do this:

_____

_____

Thoughts/Memories:

_____

_____

_____

_____

_____

_____

_____

_____

_____

_____

_____

Date Completed: _____

Description:

_____

_____

_____

_____

_____

_____

Why we wanted to do this:

_____

_____

Thoughts/Memories:

_____

_____

_____

_____

_____

_____

_____

_____

_____

_____

Date Completed: _____

Description:

_____
_____
_____
_____
_____
_____

Why we wanted to do this:

_____
_____

Thoughts/Memories:

_____
_____
_____
_____
_____
_____
_____
_____
_____
_____
_____

Date Completed: _____

Description:

_____

_____

_____

_____

_____

_____

Why we wanted to do this:

_____

_____

Thoughts/Memories:

_____

_____

_____

_____

_____

_____

_____

_____

_____

_____

_____

Date Completed:

Description:

_____

_____

_____

_____

_____

_____

Why we wanted to do this:

_____

_____

Thoughts/Memories:

_____

_____

_____

_____

_____

_____

_____

_____

_____

_____

_____

_____

>>>————————➤ >>>————————➤   >>>————————➤   >>>————————➤

Date Completed: _____

Description:

_____

_____

_____

_____

_____

_____

Why we wanted to do this:

_____

_____

Thoughts/Memories:

_____

_____

_____

_____

_____

_____

_____

_____

_____

_____

_____

Date Completed: _____

Description:

_____

_____

_____

_____

_____

_____

Why we wanted to do this:

_____

_____

Thoughts/Memories:

_____

_____

_____

_____

_____

_____

_____

_____

_____

_____

_____

Date Completed: _____

Description:

_____

_____

_____

_____

_____

Why we wanted to do this:

_____

_____

Thoughts/Memories:

_____

_____

_____

_____

_____

_____

_____

_____

_____

_____

Date Completed: _____

Description:

_____

_____

_____

_____

_____

Why we wanted to do this:

_____

_____

Thoughts/Memories:

_____

_____

_____

_____

_____

_____

_____

_____

_____

_____

_____

_____

>>>——————→ >>>——————→ >>>——————→ >>>——————→

Date Completed: _____

Description:

_____

_____

_____

_____

_____

_____

Why we wanted to do this:

_____

_____

Thoughts/Memories:

_____

_____

_____

_____

_____

_____

_____

_____

_____

_____

_____

Date Completed: _____

Description:

_____

_____

_____

_____

_____

Why we wanted to do this:

_____

_____

Thoughts/Memories:

_____

_____

_____

_____

_____

_____

_____

_____

_____

_____

Date Completed: _____

Description:

_____

_____

_____

_____

_____

_____

Why we wanted to do this:

_____

_____

Thoughts/Memories:

_____

_____

_____

_____

_____

_____

_____

_____

_____

_____

_____

Date Completed: _____

Description:

_____

_____

_____

_____

_____

Why we wanted to do this:

_____

_____

Thoughts/Memories:

_____

_____

_____

_____

_____

_____

_____

_____

_____

_____

_____

>>>———————→ >>>———————→ >>>———————→ >>>———————→

Date Completed: _____

Description:

_____

_____

_____

_____

_____

Why we wanted to do this:

_____

_____

Thoughts/Memories:

_____

_____

_____

_____

_____

_____

_____

_____

_____

_____

Date Completed: _____

Description:

_____

_____

_____

_____

_____

Why we wanted to do this:

_____

_____

Thoughts/Memories:

_____

_____

_____

_____

_____

_____

_____

_____

_____

_____

_____

_____

>>>———➤ >>>———➤ >>>———➤ >>>———➤

Date Completed: _____

Description:

_____

_____

_____

_____

_____

_____

Why we wanted to do this:

_____

_____

Thoughts/Memories:

_____

_____

_____

_____

_____

_____

_____

_____

_____

_____

_____

Date Completed: _____

Description:

_____

_____

_____

_____

_____

Why we wanted to do this:

_____

_____

Thoughts/Memories:

_____

_____

_____

_____

_____

_____

_____

_____

_____

_____

_____

Date Completed: _____

Description:

_____

_____

_____

_____

_____

Why we wanted to do this:

_____

_____

Thoughts/Memories:

_____

_____

_____

_____

_____

_____

_____

_____

_____

_____

_____

Date Completed: _____

Description:

_____

_____

_____

_____

_____

Why we wanted to do this:

_____

_____

Thoughts/Memories:

_____

_____

_____

_____

_____

_____

_____

_____

_____

_____

_____

>>>———————➤ >>>———————➤ >>>———————➤ >>>———————➤

Date Completed: _____

Description:

_____

_____

_____

_____

_____

Why we wanted to do this:

_____

_____

Thoughts/Memories:

_____

_____

_____

_____

_____

_____

_____

_____

_____

_____

_____

Date Completed: _____

Description:

_____

_____

_____

_____

_____

Why we wanted to do this:

_____

_____

Thoughts/Memories:

_____

_____

_____

_____

_____

_____

_____

_____

_____

_____

_____

>>> ———————➤   >>> ———————➤   >>> ———————➤   >>> ———————➤

Date Completed: _____

Description:

_____

_____

_____

_____

_____

_____

Why we wanted to do this:

_____

_____

Thoughts/Memories:

_____

_____

_____

_____

_____

_____

_____

_____

_____

_____

_____

Date Completed: _____

Description:

_____

_____

_____

_____

_____

Why we wanted to do this:

_____

_____

Thoughts/Memories:

_____

_____

_____

_____

_____

_____

_____

_____

_____

_____

_____

Date Completed: _____

Description:

_____

_____

_____

_____

_____

_____

Why we wanted to do this:

_____

_____

Thoughts/Memories:

_____

_____

_____

_____

_____

_____

_____

_____

_____

_____

_____

_____

Date Completed: _____

Description:

_____

_____

_____

_____

_____

Why we wanted to do this:

_____

_____

Thoughts/Memories:

_____

_____

_____

_____

_____

_____

_____

_____

_____

_____

>>>———➤ >>>———➤ >>>———➤ >>>———➤

Date Completed: _____

Description:

_____

_____

_____

_____

_____

_____

Why we wanted to do this:

_____

_____

Thoughts/Memories:

_____

_____

_____

_____

_____

_____

_____

_____

_____

_____

_____

Date Completed: _____

Description:

_____

_____

_____

_____

_____

Why we wanted to do this:

_____

_____

Thoughts/Memories:

_____

_____

_____

_____

_____

_____

_____

_____

_____

_____

_____

Date Completed: _____

Description:

_____

_____

_____

_____

_____

Why we wanted to do this:

_____

_____

Thoughts/Memories:

_____

_____

_____

_____

_____

_____

_____

_____

_____

_____

_____

Date Completed:

Description:

_____

_____

_____

_____

_____

Why we wanted to do this:

_____

_____

Thoughts/Memories:

_____

_____

_____

_____

_____

_____

_____

_____

_____

_____

_____

Date Completed: _____

Description:

_____

_____

_____

_____

_____

_____

Why we wanted to do this:

_____

_____

Thoughts/Memories:

_____

_____

_____

_____

_____

_____

_____

_____

_____

_____

_____

_____

Date Completed: _____

Description:

_____
_____
_____
_____
_____
_____

Why we wanted to do this:

_____
_____

Thoughts/Memories:

_____
_____
_____
_____
_____
_____
_____
_____
_____
_____
_____

Date Completed: _____

Description:

_____

_____

_____

_____

_____

_____

Why we wanted to do this:

_____

_____

Thoughts/Memories:

_____

_____

_____

_____

_____

_____

_____

_____

_____

_____

_____

Date Completed: _____

Description:

_____

_____

_____

_____

_____

_____

Why we wanted to do this:

_____

_____

Thoughts/Memories:

_____

_____

_____

_____

_____

_____

_____

_____

_____

_____

_____

Date Completed: _____

Description:

_____

_____

_____

_____

_____

Why we wanted to do this:

_____

_____

Thoughts/Memories:

_____

_____

_____

_____

_____

_____

_____

_____

_____

_____

_____

Date Completed: _____

Description:

_____

_____

_____

_____

_____

Why we wanted to do this:

_____

_____

Thoughts/Memories:

_____

_____

_____

_____

_____

_____

_____

_____

_____

_____

_____

_____

>>>————————→ >>>————————→ >>>————————→ >>>————————→

Date Completed: _____

Description:

_____
_____
_____
_____
_____
_____

Why we wanted to do this:

_____
_____

Thoughts/Memories:

_____
_____
_____
_____
_____
_____
_____
_____
_____
_____
_____
_____

Date Completed: _____

Description:

_____

_____

_____

_____

_____

Why we wanted to do this:

_____

_____

Thoughts/Memories:

_____

_____

_____

_____

_____

_____

_____

_____

_____

_____

>>>——————→ >>>——————→ >>>——————→ >>>——————→

Date Completed: _____

Description:

_____

_____

_____

_____

_____

_____

Why we wanted to do this:

_____

_____

Thoughts/Memories:

_____

_____

_____

_____

_____

_____

_____

_____

_____

_____

_____

Date Completed: _____

Description:

_____

_____

_____

_____

_____

Why we wanted to do this:

_____

_____

Thoughts/Memories:

_____

_____

_____

_____

_____

_____

_____

_____

_____

_____

_____

Date Completed: _____

Description:

_____

_____

_____

_____

_____

Why we wanted to do this:

_____

_____

Thoughts/Memories:

_____

_____

_____

_____

_____

_____

_____

_____

_____

_____

_____

Date Completed: _____

Description:

_____

_____

_____

_____

_____

Why we wanted to do this:

_____

_____

Thoughts/Memories:

_____

_____

_____

_____

_____

_____

_____

_____

_____

_____

_____

_____

>>>———→ >>>———→ >>>———→ >>>———→

Date Completed: _____

Description:

_____
_____
_____
_____
_____
_____

Why we wanted to do this:

_____
_____

Thoughts/Memories:

_____
_____
_____
_____
_____
_____
_____
_____
_____
_____

Date Completed: _____

Description:

_____

_____

_____

_____

_____

_____

Why we wanted to do this:

_____

_____

Thoughts/Memories:

_____

_____

_____

_____

_____

_____

_____

_____

_____

_____

_____

Date Completed: _____

Description:

_____

_____

_____

_____

_____

_____

Why we wanted to do this:

_____

_____

Thoughts/Memories:

_____

_____

_____

_____

_____

_____

_____

_____

_____

_____

_____

_____

Date Completed: _____

Description:

_____

_____

_____

_____

_____

_____

Why we wanted to do this:

_____

_____

Thoughts/Memories:

_____

_____

_____

_____

_____

_____

_____

_____

_____

_____

_____

>>>———➤ >>>———➤ >>>———➤ >>>———➤

Date Completed: _____

Description:

_____

_____

_____

_____

_____

Why we wanted to do this:

_____

_____

Thoughts/Memories:

_____

_____

_____

_____

_____

_____

_____

_____

_____

_____

_____

Date Completed: _____

Description:

_____

_____

_____

_____

_____

_____

Why we wanted to do this:

_____

_____

Thoughts/Memories:

_____

_____

_____

_____

_____

_____

_____

_____

_____

_____

_____

>>> ———→ >>> ———→ >>> ———→ >>> ———→

Date Completed: _____

Description:

_____

_____

_____

_____

_____

_____

Why we wanted to do this:

_____

_____

Thoughts/Memories:

_____

_____

_____

_____

_____

_____

_____

_____

_____

_____

_____

Date Completed: _____

Description:

_____

_____

_____

_____

_____

_____

Why we wanted to do this:

_____

_____

Thoughts/Memories:

_____

_____

_____

_____

_____

_____

_____

_____

_____

_____

_____

Date Completed: _____

Description:

_____

_____

_____

_____

_____

Why we wanted to do this:

_____

_____

Thoughts/Memories:

_____

_____

_____

_____

_____

_____

_____

_____

_____

_____

_____

>>> ———➤ >>> ———➤   >>> ———➤ >>> ———➤

Date Completed: _____

Description:

_____

_____

_____

_____

_____

_____

Why we wanted to do this:

_____

_____

Thoughts/Memories:

_____

_____

_____

_____

_____

_____

_____

_____

_____

_____

>>>———————→ >>>———————→ >>>———————→ >>>———————→

Date Completed: _____

Description:

_____

_____

_____

_____

_____

_____

Why we wanted to do this:

_____

_____

Thoughts/Memories:

_____

_____

_____

_____

_____

_____

_____

_____

_____

_____

_____

Date Completed: _____

Description:

_____
_____
_____
_____
_____
_____

Why we wanted to do this:

_____
_____

Thoughts/Memories:

_____
_____
_____
_____
_____
_____
_____
_____
_____
_____
_____
_____

>>>———————→ >>>———————→ >>>———————→ >>>———————→

Date Completed: _____

Description:

_____

_____

_____

_____

_____

_____

Why we wanted to do this:

_____

_____

Thoughts/Memories:

_____

_____

_____

_____

_____

_____

_____

_____

_____

_____

_____

>>> ———➤ >>> ———➤ >>> ———➤ >>> ———➤

Date Completed: _____

Description:

_____

_____

_____

_____

_____

Why we wanted to do this:

_____

_____

Thoughts/Memories:

_____

_____

_____

_____

_____

_____

_____

_____

_____

_____

>>>———————>   >>>———————>   >>>———————>   >>>———————>

Date Completed: _____

Description:

_____

_____

_____

_____

_____

Why we wanted to do this:

_____

_____

Thoughts/Memories:

_____

_____

_____

_____

_____

_____

_____

_____

_____

_____

_____

13540427R00063

Made in the USA
Lexington, KY
01 November 2018